# Ellis Island

**Terry Allan Hicks**

**Marshall Cavendish**
Benchmark

Marshall Cavendish Benchmark
99 White Plains Road
Tarrytown, New York 10591-9001
www.marshallcavendish.us

Library of Congress Cataloging-in-Publication Data
Hicks, Terry Allan.
Ellis Island / by Terry Allan Hicks.
p. cm. — (Symbols of America)
Summary: "An exploration of the island that served as a gateway to thousands of immigrants and that has since become an important American symbol"—Provided by publisher.
Includes bibliographical references and index.
ISBN-13: 978-0-7614-2134-4
ISBN-10: 0-7614-2134-3
1. Ellis Island Immigration Station (N.Y. and N.J.)—Juvenile literature.
2. United States—Emigration and immigration—History—Juvenile literature.
I. Title. II. Series.

JV6484.H53 2006
304.8'73—dc22
2005020610

Photo research by Anne Burns Images

Front cover: Corbis/Bill Ross
Back cover: U.S. Postal Service

The photographs in this book are used by permission and through the courtesy of: *National Park Service/Liberty National Monument:* 1, 7, 8, 5, 9, 20, 23, 24, 27, 28, 35. *North Wind Picture Archives:* 4, 11, 16. *State Historical Society of Wisconsin:* 12. *Brown Brothers:* 31. *Corbis:* Andrew Holbrooke, 32.

Series design by Adam Mietlowski

Printed in Malaysia

1 3 5 6 4 2

# Contents

# CHAPTER ONE

# The Golden Door

For millions of people, the American dream began on a little island in New York Harbor. They came as *immigrants,* people who had left their homelands, often forever. They were searching for a better life in America.

In the late 1800s and early 1900s, it sometimes seemed as if the entire world was on the move. More than half of the world's immigrants came to the United States—so many that in some parts of the world, "America Fever" was said to be sweeping over the land. People were eager to come to the United States. Most of them entered America through the great immigration station on Ellis Island.

*An immigrant family waits its turn at Ellis Island in 1901.*

These immigrants had suffered great *hardship* to make their dreams a reality. Many of them had sold everything they owned to pay for their passage to America. During their journey, they had spent long, miserable days and nights "below decks," crowded with hundreds of other people in dark, cramped *compartments* and cargo holds.

*A famous 1907 photograph shows passengers "below decks" on a German ship headed for New York.* ▶

Now, at last, they had arrived in America. As they crowded on deck, pressing against the railing, they gasped at the sight of New York's skyscrapers, off in the distance. They stared at the newly built Statue of Liberty.

Why were so many people willing to give up everything they owned, everything they knew, to begin again in America? Many, such as the Jews of Russia and the Armenians of Turkey, were seeking freedom from religious and ethnic *persecution*. Others, such as the Irish, were fleeing terrible *poverty*. But all these immigrants had one thing in common: a burning desire for greater *opportunity*.

◀ *The Statue of Liberty was often one of the first sights immigrants had of their new homeland.*

The United States was growing fast. Its factories, farms, and mines offered plenty of work, even for laborers who spoke little or no English and who had few skills. The immigrants often faced harsh conditions, working long hours for little pay. Still, they built new lives for themselves and their children. Most importantly, with their variety of languages, their religions, and their traditions, they changed America forever.

*This illustration shows young women laboring in a Massachusetts textile mill. Through hard work and savings, families tried to improve their lives.*

So many people entered America through the immigration station on Ellis Island that it came to be called the "Golden Door." Many people who would be famous someday—artists and inventors, movie stars and political leaders—passed through Ellis Island on their way to a new life in America.

*Immigrants leave Ellis Island in 1917 to find new homes in America.*

# CHAPTER TWO

# The Gateway to America

For most of the late 1800s, foreigners who entered America through New York passed through the Castle Garden immigration station in Manhattan. But by the 1890s, so many immigrants were arriving that Castle Garden could no longer handle them all. So the government decided to build a new immigration station on Ellis Island.

*The Castle Garden immigration station, shown in the 1840s.*

Ellis Island was originally called Kioshk (Gull) Island by the Mohegan Indians, after the birds that gathered there in search of oysters. When the Dutch and later the English settled the area, it was known as Oyster Island. Later, it was called Gibbet Island because captured pirates were hanged there on a *gibbet,* or gallows.

The island takes its present name from Samuel Ellis. He built a tavern there in the 1700s. In 1808, the War Department bought the island for $10,000. It was used to hold British prisoners during the War of 1812 and later to store gunpowder.

◀ *During the Civil War, the United States Navy kept gunpowder on the island, in storehouses called magazines.*

The Ellis Island immigration station opened on January 1, 1892. A fire badly damaged the original wooden buildings in June 1897. They were replaced by the beautiful brick–and–limestone structures that still stand today. In the main building immigrants and their documents were *examined*. The station also included a kitchen and dining area, a laundry, a hospital for those who arrived ill, and a *morgue* for those who did not survive the long, hard journey across the Atlantic Ocean.

**Where Did They Come From? (1892-1954)**

Great Britain and Ireland: 3.5 million
Italy: 3.3 million
Poland: 1.5 million
France, Spain, Portugal, and the Netherlands: 1.1 million total
Germany: 1.1 million
Russia, Lithuania, and Ukraine: 750,000 total
Greece: 518,000
Austria: 500,000
Armenia, Palestine, Turkey, and Syria: 200,000 total
Czechoslovakia: 170,000
Hungary: 165,000
Romania: 155,000

*Ellis Island as it looked in 1906.* ▶

When immigrants arrived in New York Harbor, barges and ferries took them from their ships to the immigration station. Sometimes so many ships were crowded into the harbor at one time that 20,000 people—the population of a small city—were waiting for barges to the island.

◀ *A long line of immigrants waiting patiently to pass through Ellis Island in the early 1900s.*

Once on the island, the immigrants left their *belongings* in the Baggage Room on the lower level of the main building. Then they walked up a wide staircase into the huge Registry Room on the second floor. A great crowd of people would usually be waiting there already. On one day in 1907, 11,747 people passed through the Registry Room.

*Hundreds of people are shown crowded into the Registry Room (also known as the Great Hall) in 1917.*

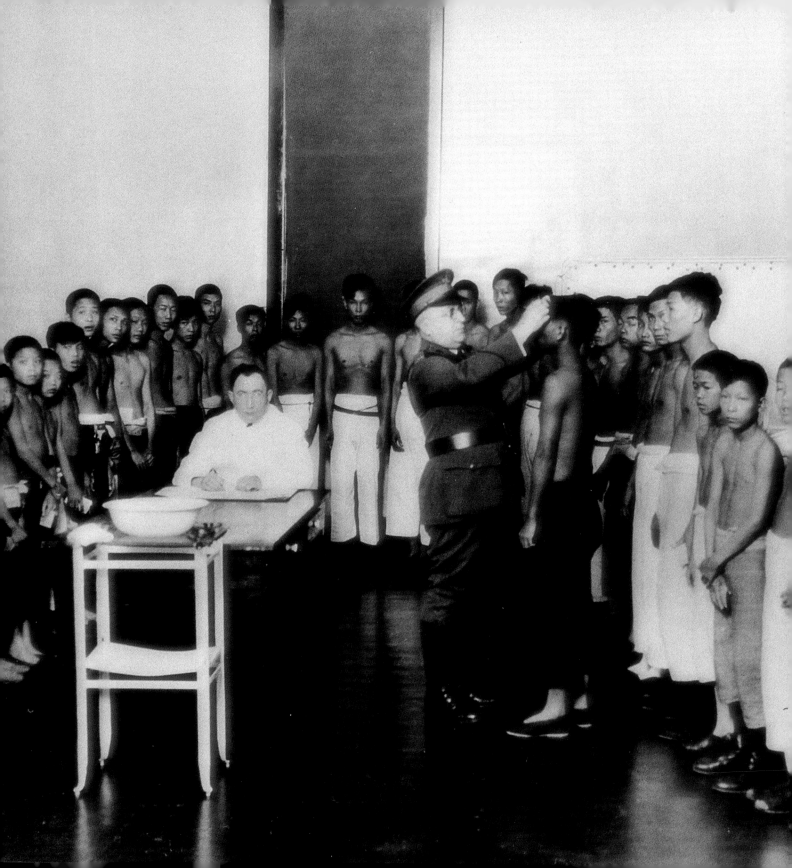

The next step was a visit to a doctor. This usually lasted only a few seconds. Then came an interview. Officials had to be certain the immigrants were who they said they were and had the right to enter the country. Beginning in 1917, immigrants also had to prove they could read. They usually did this by reciting a passage from the Bible in their native languages.

*These new arrivals from the South Pacific are being given a medical examination.*

These *inspections* usually took from two to three hours. After that, most immigrants were free to leave Ellis Island and begin their new lives in America. Some, however, were not allowed to remain because of problems with their health or their documents. About 2 percent of the people who arrived at Ellis Island, about 250,000 people, had to return to their homelands, sometimes leaving their families behind in America. Their sad stories caused the immigration station to be given another name: "The Island of Tears."

*A group of children in Ellis Island's hospital, in the years before World War One.* ▶

The first immigrant to enter the United States through Ellis Island on that January morning in 1892 was fifteen-year-old Annie Moore. She had traveled from Ireland on the steamship *Nevada*. She was given a ten-dollar gold coin to mark the occasion. Then she went to join her family, who had immigrated several years earlier. Twelve million people followed her over the next six decades. Today, more than 100 million Americans have at least one *ancestor* who passed through the Golden Door between 1892 and 1954. This is about 42 percent of the population of the United States.

**Did You Know?**

Another immigration station, Angel Island in San Francisco Bay, is sometimes called the "Ellis Island of the West." It was built in 1910—as a way of keeping Chinese immigrants *out* of the United States.

*Annie Moore, fourteen years after her arrival in America, with her young child.*

# CHAPTER THREE

# Ellis Island Today

By the 1920s, fewer immigrants were entering the United States. Ellis Island's days as the gateway to America were coming to an end. During World War Two, the government used the island as a prison to hold people from countries the United States was fighting.

*A teacher leads a group of children in exercises in 1921.*

On November 12, 1954, Ellis Island was officially closed. The government tried to sell the site, but no one was interested. The buildings began to crumble, and Ellis Island was all but forgotten.

Over the years, however, Ellis Island slowly regained its place in America's memory. On May 11, 1965, President Lyndon Johnson named Ellis Island part of the Statue of Liberty National Monument. Then, in 1974, the Restore Ellis Island Committee was formed to raise money to restore the site and open an immigration museum.

◀ *By the 1980s, much of Ellis Island was in ruins.*

It was the largest project of its kind in American history. The *restoration* began in 1984. On September 10, 1990, the Ellis Island Immigration Museum opened its doors. Today, the museum is one of the most popular tourist attractions in New York City. About two million visitors come every year. They see the clothing, baggage, and documents that the immigrants brought with them. Visitors can also look at photographs and films of the people arriving at Ellis Island. Many people come to search through Ellis Island's huge *archives* for their own family names. Others come simply to remember and honor the great *sacrifices* their ancestors made in search of a new life in America.

*One of the many exhibits that can be seen today at the Ellis Island Immigration Museum.*

# Glossary

**ancestor**—A family member from the past; a relative someone is descended from.

**archives**—A place where documents or other important records are kept.

**belongings**—The items that people own.

**compartment**—A small area for passengers or storing goods.

**examine**—To look at or inspect.

**gibbet**—A place where criminals were once hanged.

**hardship**—Difficulty, suffering, or tough times.

**immigrant**—Someone who leaves a country to live somewhere else.

**inspection**—An examination or review to be sure someone or something is healthy or acceptable.

**morgue**—A place where dead bodies are kept before burial.

**opportunity**—The chance to do something.

**persecution**—Abuse or harmful, often violent, treatment.

**poverty**—The lack of money or other necessities of life.

**restoration**—The act of repairing, rebuilding, or improving a structure or place.

**sacrifice**—Something that is given up in the hope of improving one's life or conditions.

# Find Out More

## Books

Binns, Tristan Boyer. *Ellis Island.* Chicago: Heinemann, 2001.

Coan, Peter Morton. *Ellis Island Interviews: In Their Own Words.* New York: Facts on File, 1997.

Jango-Cohen, Judith. *Ellis Island.* Danbury, CT: Children's Press, 2005.

Levine, Ellen. —*if Your Name Was Changed at Ellis Island.* New York: Scholastic, 1993.

Marcovitz, Hal. *Ellis Island.* Broomall, PA: Mason Crest, 2002.

Quiri, Patricia Ryon. *Ellis Island.* Danbury, CT: Children's Press, 1998.

Raatma, Lucia. *Ellis Island.* Mankato, MN: Compass Point, 2002.

Yans-McLaughlin, Virginia, and Marjorie Lightman, with the Statue of Liberty Ellis Island Foundation. *Ellis Island and the Peopling of America.* New York: New Press, 1997.

## Web Sites

Ellis Island Immigration Museum
http://www.ellisisland.com/

"Ellis Island" on the History Channel
http://www.historychannel.com/ellisisland/index2.html

National Park Service—Ellis Island for Kids
http://www.nps.gov/elis/pphtml/forkids.html

The Statue of Liberty—Ellis Island Foundation
http://www.ellisisland.org/

# Index